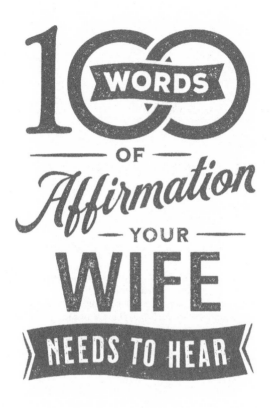

Matt Jacobson

Revell
a division of Baker Publishing Group
Grand Rapids, Michigan

Published by Revell
a division of Baker Publishing Group
PO Box 6287, Grand Rapids, MI 49516-6287
www.revellbooks.com

Printed in the United States of America

Library of Congress Cataloging-in-Publication Data
Names: Jacobson, Matthew L., author. | Jacobson, Lisa, author.
Title: 100 words of affirmation your wife needs to hear / Matthew L. Jacobson
   and Lisa Jacobson.
Other titles: One hundred words of affirmation your wife needs to hear
Description: Grand Rapids : Revell, a division of Baker Publishing Group,
   2019.
Identifiers: LCCN 2018052087 | ISBN 9780800736644
Subjects: LCSH: Husbands—Religious life. | Wives—Psychology. | Man-
   woman relationships—Religious aspects—Christianity. | Man-woman
   relationships—Psychological aspects. | Marriage—Religious aspects—
   Christianity. | Affirmations.
Classification: LCC BV4528.3 .J33 2019 | DDC 248.8/425—dc23
LC record available at https://lccn.loc.gov/2018052087

Unless otherwise indicated, Scripture quotations are from the King James
Version of the Bible.

Scripture quotations labeled NKJV are from the New King
James Version®. Copyright © 1982 by Thomas Nelson.
Used by permission. All rights reserved.

In keeping with biblical principles of
creation stewardship, Baker Publishing Group advocates the responsible
use of our natural resources. As a
member of the Green Press Initia-
tive, our company uses recycled
paper when possible. The text paper
of this book is composed in part of
post-consumer waste.

19 20 21 22 23 24 25   7 6 5 4 3 2 1

Introduction

She wants to know what you think, but she especially wants to know what you think of her.

Do you value her? Care how she feels? Respect her? Honor her? Feel close to her? Need her?

As husbands, we can think and feel all these things deeply and still never say them, never tell her how we feel *about her*.

And there are the other voices that will never be silent—the voice inside your wife's head, the voice speaking from every clothing ad, the voice calling from every corner of society, telling her, "You're not good enough." "You don't measure up." "You're too much this." "You're not enough that."

They're convincing voices that tear her down and diminish her.

But your voice is powerful too and far more important to your wife's heart than anything this world has to say. That's why it's important for you to use your power to speak affirming words into your wife's heart today, tomorrow, and every day God gives you together.

Maybe it's difficult for you to find the words. In this simple, powerful book are one hundred words to help you get started affirming your wife's great importance and value to you and the people she loves.

Do this and you will discover what every happy, fulfilled husband has learned: the husband who sincerely and consistently fills his wife's heart with affirming words of love soon discovers that she returns to him far more than he ever poured into her soul.

You give *a lot*, and I deeply appreciate how much you give.

Virtually every wife and mother feels like she is constantly meeting the needs of others. *Your wife* feels like she is constantly meeting the needs of others because she is, especially if there are young kids in the house. And she's always there for you too . . . giving.

Genuinely showing appreciation for her through sincere words is a powerful way a wise husband ensures that as she is pouring out, she doesn't begin to feel empty. Gratitude is so powerful, but it's only meaningful when it's expressed. By themselves, your deep feelings of gratitude for your wife do not mean all that much. Don't let this day pass before you let her know.

2

You are *beautiful.*

The message the world constantly offers up to your wife is exactly the opposite: "You're not beautiful." "You're not very smart." "You don't accomplish much." "You don't have much value."

And it's hard for her not to believe those relentless messages. That's why she needs to hear from you regularly on the topic—and not with some flippant, offhand, throwaway comment, but a message that comes straight from your heart.

Take your wife in your arms. Look directly into her eyes for a moment, and then tell her how beautiful she is to you.

You make me want to be a BETTER MAN.

Every honest husband knows that without his wife, he wouldn't be the man he is. But does your wife know this is how *you* feel? Sometimes we treat our wives like they are mind readers, but your wife can't read your mind and she can't know what's in your heart unless you communicate these things to her.

Remember this verse from Luke 6: "A good man out of the good treasure of his heart brings forth good; and an evil man out of the evil treasure of his heart brings forth evil. For out of the abundance of the heart his mouth speaks" (v. 45 NKJV).

Tell your wife what is in your heart. Let her know the powerful and pivotal role she plays in the man you've become and the man you desire to be because of her.

I want to *thank you* for your *faithfulness* to our family.

Being a wife and mother is a day-in and day-out, 24/7, 365-day job. And yet there she is—providing a safe and peaceful place, putting her heart into her home, being faithful when no one is looking (or patting her on the back or giving her a raise) . . . for years.

Tell her you are genuinely grateful for her steady faithfulness to the home and life you are building together.

Yes, I *fantasize*
all the time ... about you!

She knows you are tempted. She knows you get "offers" of various kinds. She is all too aware of this sex-soaked, filth-saturated world you both inhabit. And she wonders, *What is he feeling? What is he thinking? What is his thought life like? Does he fantasize about sex?*

First of all, there is no room—absolutely no room—for anything but total faithfulness to your wife. Anything less than total faithfulness is unfaithfulness. For those who might wonder whether a given activity (with the body or the mind) is being unfaithful, just ask yourself, *If my wife discovered me doing this by chance, would I feel ashamed? Would she feel honored?* Got your answer?

So, no worries. Let your imagination go, because there's nothing wrong with thinking about sex ... *with your wife.* Tell her (1) she is the only focus of your sexual interest ... you think about her all the time and (2) she is the only outlet for your sexual passion.

Give your wife the beautiful peace of knowing you are faithful, even in the secret places of your thought life.

I've
l e a r n e d   a   l o t
from you.

It takes a humble man to admit that he has a lot to learn. It also takes a smart man to recognize—and acknowledge—that he has learned a lot from his wife, this most amazing gift God gave you to complete you and make you better in every way. Let's be real—her wise advice has kept you out of a whole lot of trouble, hasn't it? (At least the times you listened to her!)

And, finally, it takes a good man to make sure he has communicated to his wife how much he has learned and continues to learn from her. Being honest with your wife in this way is a deep blessing to her.

I've seen you *grow* so much.

Your wife desires to grow as a person, to become more mature, stronger, deeper, better, and more in tune with God's design and desire. She's grown a great deal since you've been married, but the everydayness of life can obscure that fact, especially for her.

Sometimes we don't see the things that are directly in front of us. Sometimes we're too close to notice significant change. It's not unlike relatives who visit once a year. "Wow, Johnny!" they might say. "You sure have grown!" Johnny's growth was so incremental that his immediate family hardly took notice. We can be like that with our wives. So find a moment. Take stock of the tremendous, beautiful growth and maturity you've observed in your wife and celebrate by letting her know you see these things in her.

I *love* your body.

There is something powerful and peace-giving in the message to your wife that, physically, she is wonderful just the way she is. She doesn't have to change and she doesn't have to be something she currently isn't to be perfect for you in every way.

This is a vital message your wife can't get from any other source. Maybe she's just stepping out of the shower. Maybe she's dressing for an evening out. Maybe she's standing over some boiling potatoes on the stove. Look for the moment when you can give her a reassuring hug and tell her you like the way her body looks and feels.

I like
s p e n d i n g   t i m e
with you.

Every one of us wishes for people to want to hang out with us—and for no other reason than they just like to be with us. Every one of us wants to be wanted. Your wife is no different. She doesn't want you to "fulfill your duty" and spend an hour with her doing errands because you feel obligated. She wants to know that you enjoy her company.

Taking each other for granted is one of the many things in marriage that is so easy to do. And many men, when asked by their wives, "Do you even want to spend time with me?" respond indignantly, "Of course. Where did you even get that idea?" How about from your countenance, your behavior (when was the last time you initiated being together without an agenda or a to-do list?), or the fact that you've never communicated directly how you enjoy her company?

Smile with your eyes and tell your wife, "I like spending time with you!" Then ask her if she is free on Saturday afternoon (or whenever) for a couple of hours to go out for coffee, lunch, or dinner; go for a walk in the park; go to the art museum; go on a bike ride; scuba dive down to the shark cage to see great white sharks up close (okay, maybe not that one but you get the idea!). Say it, then prove it. It's so simple and it means so much to her heart.

You're FUN
to be with.

Remember those first years of marriage? You used to laugh a lot together. You had a great deal of fun back then. But life has a way of sucking the fun right out of marriage, doesn't it? It doesn't have to be that way. As the husband, you have a large responsibility to make sure you are finding the time and creating the circumstances for the two of you to have some fun together.

This week, take charge. Don't let life use up all your available time and prevent the two of you from spending a little of that time together. Help your wife set aside all the demands on her energy and responsibilities that never stop. Pick a few hours some day before the week's end. Tell her, "You're fun to be with," and then prove it by sharing your idea for a three-hour getaway with her.

What a *fantastic* meal!

When she asks, "What do you think of the casserole?" no wife wants her husband to start analyzing the meal like some forensic scientist dissecting a corpse for a murder trial. In fact, she's not really asking about the meal at all. Peel away the layers and you'll see she's actually asking whether you feel she measures up as a wife. Different meal, same question . . . doesn't matter because it's the same questions every time—*Do I measure up? Did I do a good job? Are you pleased?*

When your wife cooks you something and puts it on the table, it may look like a stir-fry, but she's actually serving you her heart—it's her heart on a platter. How you handle yourself in these moments may mean the difference between never getting another home-cooked meal and seeing her blossom into someone who would give a five-star chef a run for their money.

The man who criticizes his wife's efforts in the kitchen is an idiot—sorry, guys, but I call it like I see it. It's like breaking your leg to improve your skiing ability—brilliant!

Oh, and for the husband who is just helping with "a little constructive criticism," listen and learn: There's no such thing as constructive criticism when your wife is serving you dinner. It's all destructive because all she hears is criticism.

There are very few meals in marriage (and these days guys do a lot of cooking, or grilling, like me on my Traeger!) about which there isn't something positive and encouraging to say. Even if you're eating a burnt casserole, you can say, "I'm sorry this didn't turn out, but I know and appreciate the love that went into making it."

Will you *forgive* me?

Wouldn't it be great if after saying "I do!" and exchanging rings, you never made another mistake, never did something to hurt your wife, or never chose to sin for the rest of your life?

But marriage doesn't really work out like that, or hasn't worked out like that, has it? When men sin against their wives, many of them take the coward's way out. And what is that? They say a simple "I'm sorry" and move on quickly. This isn't good enough, and it's not really repenting. It's more like ducking for cover. (You've never done that, have you?)

To walk in true repentance with your wife, openly and humbly acknowledge your offense without qualifying statements (justification) as to why you did what you did. With a sincere tone, express your sorrow for what you did and how it made your spouse feel. Never say, "I'm sorry you feel that way." And remember, saying "I'm sorry" is never enough. You have to humbly ask, "Will you please forgive me for (name the offense)?"

13

Thanks for your diligence in running this house.

Economists estimate that to replace a wife and mother running a home would cost well over $100,000 a year. Why? Because she does a whole lot!

These days, men are much more involved than in previous generations. Even so, wives (even those working outside the home) tend to do the bulk of household work and management.

How powerful it is to hear a word of encouragement for what is a relentless, 365-days-a-year job. The wise husband won't let her work go unnoticed (and doesn't leave it all on her shoulders either). And the smart father leads the way in teaching his children to help with the housework and to deeply value and verbally appreciate all mom does.

You can tell her, "Yes, my beautiful, wonderful wife, thank you so much for your faithful diligence in running this home!"

Our kids are so *fortunate* to have you as their mother.

If you have children, you know you do a whole lot of giving and, especially in the early years, they do a lot of taking, with no reciprocation. That's okay, because that's how God designed it. Even so, the oft thankless job of "mom" should not be thankless. That year-in, year-out faithfulness is adding up to something beautiful—something that will matter deeply in the lives of those God has entrusted to the two of you.

But in the moment, when there are dirty diapers to change and infants to feed, it can be hard for your wife to see that far down the road. It's up to you to speak hope for the future into your wife's heart. Remind her often that your children are so fortunate to have her as their mom.

God wanted me to be *happy* . . . that's why He made you my wife.

Let the theologians debate if God really wants us to be happy. This isn't a theological position, just a recognition that God is a good Father who knows how to give good gifts—and your wife is one of them. The fact is, God has blessed you through the gift of your wife. By saying this to her, you're affirming her value as a gift from God and as someone who brings joy to your life.

You bring out
the *best* in me.

It's a simple phrase that marks the moment when your
wife kept you from acting rashly; helped you see something more clearly, make a better decision, or communicate more effectively; or reminded you of an obligation you
needed to fulfill.

Lisa will often ask me a question such as, "Is that what
you meant to communicate?" or "Are you sure doing such
and such will achieve your desired ends?" or "Do you think
that is the right approach with the kids?" In each case, I get
to evaluate, consider, and often alter course.

Our wives bring out the best in us. We should let them
know!

You are a
fantastic person.

Voices . . . there are about a zillion of them whispering to your wife every day, and sadly, most of them are very negative. They're untrue, but that doesn't make them any less powerful. She needs to hear this from you: "You are a fantastic person!" Use your powerful voice to help your wife see the truth about herself.

You are a
DEEP RIVER.

My wife is a deep person—something that just about every good man recognizes about his own wife. There's a lot going on in her mind and heart—serious and substantive thoughts, important plans, and strong desires. From time to time, she will find it encouraging when you openly acknowledge her depth, her substance—the reality that she is a person with deep thoughts and a lot to offer you. In doing so, you will fill your wife with a sense of your respect and will, in turn, support her self-respect.

You are as *beautiful* to me today as the day we married.

Your wife was such a beautiful bride, wasn't she? The moment she appeared, walking down the aisle, she took your breath away. Then there was time—the great ravager of all things beautiful. But the wise husband, the happy husband, the fulfilled husband settles in his mind a truth that stands in opposition to the messages of time.

Settle in your mind and heart this truth: *My wife is as beautiful to me as the day we met.* In a marriage based on genuine, deep love, this isn't a false statement we tell ourselves. It's the truth, because our marriage has grown deeper, richer, closer . . . and more beautiful in every way. By you seeing your wife through the eyes of love, she will never become less than beautiful to you. And she needs to hear this from you often. Take her in your arms and whisper in her ear, "You are as beautiful to me today as the day we married."

My *favorite place* to be is with you.

Time for a gut check: Where is your heart right now? At home with your wife or some other place, such as the office, out with the guys, or on the golf course? Many influences are tugging on the hearts of husbands, and their wives know it. They can *feel* it. And your wife knows, right down to her socks, when your heart is and when it isn't with her at home.

The next time you're walking out the door, tell her that your heart never leaves: "Even though I may be away for a bit, my heart stays right here with you."

You complete me.

It's true, your wife really is your other half. That's exactly what God says about the two of you—the two shall become one. And in God's grand plan, you were incomplete without her.

Telling your wife "You complete me" demonstrates that you recognize and value her immense place and role in your heart and life.

You make *loving* fun.

Do you enjoy having sex with your wife? Then give her a hug in the morning and tell her you enjoy being with her.

She wants to know your needs are met. She wants to know you enjoyed being with her. She wants to know she "does it" right for you.

So talk about sex with your wife. Talk about the time you had together. Let her know you had fun being with her.

I wouldn't be
half the man I am
without you.

This statement is true in so many ways. If you are walking as God intended for you both, then your wife completes you. You know this. But have you told her specifically and directly that you believe it?

Telling your wife this truth from time to time is a healthy reminder to you both of her value and worth and that what you are doing in the world is only happening because she is your wife.

You are who you are because she is your wife, and she will love to hear you say it. From your mouth to her heart.

I was wrong
and you were right.

When was the last time you and your wife saw things differently? When was the last time you went back and forth and the discussion got a little heated (pride on display), maybe even a little hot? You just *knew* you were right, and there she was, not budging an inch! But then some more light was shed on the subject—a little bit of new information—and suddenly the truth became clear to you both.

She was right and you were wrong.

And what happened then?

All too often this becomes the moment when you steer the conversation away from the discussion at hand and never mention it again. But this is wrong. This is prideful. This is sinful.

As husbands, we don't like the taste of humble pie, do we? (Does anyone?) But this is the moment to humble yourself and affirm your wife by openly and directly acknowledging to her that she was right and you were wrong.

Admitting that you are wrong feels like weakness to your flesh, but that's what's interesting about humbling yourself.

It doesn't make you weaker. It speaks to your strength—your willingness and security in yourself to admit when you are wrong and acknowledge to your wife that she was, indeed, right on this one.

Maybe you're one of those husbands who always quickly humbles himself when he is wrong. God bless you, and keep up the good work! For the rest of you, your marriage will take a big step forward when your wife comes to realize you care more about truth than about your own pride.

When you're wrong, don't waste time. Acknowledge openly and quickly that you were wrong and she was right.

I'd like to go for a walk with you . . . wanna come?

The power of this simple invitation can move mountains. So much is implied in it: *I like you. I want to be with you. I enjoy spending time with you. I like being seen with you.*

When you invite your wife to go for a walk, you are speaking a message of closeness and love to her heart. For many wives, this invitation will come as a total shock. *He wants to go on a walk with me? Wait, did something bad happen?*

Don't worry. Just go with it and show her that you really do want to hold her hand and walk together. (Hand-holding is optional but highly recommended!)

You are my
WORLD.

These can be just words or you can cultivate this idea as a
reality in your marriage. Every wife, with perfect clarity,
knows the difference between the two.

And you should cultivate this reality in your home and
your wife's heart. She should have total confidence that
you see her as central and paramount to the life you are
living.

They're only four words, but they contain a universe of
affirmation about who you are and what matters to you.

The Bible tells men: *love* your wife like Christ *loves* the Church . . . I like my job!

By saying this, you're telling your wife, "I like you, I like being married to you, and I like being with you." But help her understand you're saying a whole lot more too. You're saying that you are ready to lay down your life for her. You're ready to sacrifice for her. Bless your wife by demonstrating to her that you understand the serious requirement that God has placed squarely on your shoulders as her husband. You are a man under authority—under God's authority—and He will hold you accountable for how you followed His instruction. "Husbands, love your wives, even as Christ also loved the church, and gave himself for it" (Eph. 5:25).

I *like* going out with you ... what are you doing tonight?

Men, I wish I had a nickel for every time a wife wrote me and said that her husband almost never takes her out, that she literally can't remember the last time they went on a date. I'd be a millionaire. One (selfish, foolish) man admitted to me he has *never* taken his wife on a date. This guy has been married for fourteen years and they have a zillion kids. Lucky for him, he's married to a godly woman who has chosen not to be resentful.

Question: When was the last time you took your wife out on a date for no reason other than you desire to be with her—you desire her? No birthday, no anniversary, no promotion, no nothing except pure "I love you" romance?

And it doesn't count if she arranged the babysitting, picked the restaurant, and chose the day and time.

When was the last time you did *everything*? All she

had to do was show up at the appointed time looking beautiful?

By making the effort, you're telling her several critical things:

1) You're so worth it!
2) I love being with you!
3) I'm still in love with you!

Now, if you're doing this to "get something," you've got it all backwards. Do it because you love her. Period. And you'll enjoy what every wise, loving husband has discovered. Doing so is like pouring love into your wife's heart and you'll receive back far more from her than you ever poured into her soul.

The laundry never stops coming and you never quit. You're *amazing*, and I really appreciate it.

Maybe you're one of those guys who helps with the domestic chores, but in this enlightened age, married women (even wives who work outside the home) by far still do the laundry most of the time. It's a mundane job. It's never completed. Day after day, there it is . . . another load of laundry. When was the last time you took a moment and stopped to tell your wife how much you appreciate her doing the laundry?

Your breasts *satisfy me.*

She wants to be alluring to you. She wants to satisfy you. She wants to be enough. We know the Bible teaches that men are to be faithful in everything. We know that we are to be content with our wives. But did you know that being content with your wife, being satisfied with her, is a choice the Bible tells you to make?

Proverbs 5:19 says, "Let her breasts satisfy thee at all times; and be thou ravished always with her love."

The next time you give your wife a hug from behind, holding her breasts gently in your cupped hands, whisper in her ear, "Your breasts satisfy me."

You're so smart.

Of course your wife's intelligent. She's a very smart lady. But does she think of herself this way? Is this how she feels and what she believes? Be sure to build up your wife by letting her know you believe she's one sharp lady. Tell her that she's smart (she married you, didn't she?). Seriously, though, your wife needs to know that you don't merely love her for her looks and body; you love her person and respect her intellect.

I *value* your insight.

Your wife may have a completely different personality from you, and she may see things altogether differently from you as well. This is a massive blessing of God in your life. Value her understanding. Value her insight. Value her way of thinking that is so different from yours. All these differences enable you to be better informed, to have a clearer understanding, and to make better decisions.

When you tell your wife you value her insight, you are validating her intelligence, wisdom, and way of seeing the world. You are affirming her as a person, which is a deeply encouraging experience for her.

You have
a lot to offer.

It's true that she has a great deal to offer, but sometimes—most times—she can't see it or doesn't feel that others can see it. This is especially true for a wife whose home life before marrying you was all about put-downs and ridicule (all in good fun, of course, her family tells itself). But the damage is done and now she doubts herself.

It's the strangest thing, but the most accomplished, competent wives can be plagued with a voice from the past that says "You don't do anything right." "You're a joke." "You don't have anything to offer." "You screwed up again!" (Of course, this is often true of grown men too.)

But by God's grace there is a powerhouse in your wife's world called . . . her husband! She needs to hear these words of encouragement from you regularly because they are true, and what you say matters to her heart.

You have a lot to offer!

Your hair looks *fantastic*!

At some point, your wife is going to come home from the salon where she just had her hair done, and she will hope you'll notice on your own. If you do, there's only one correct response: "Your hair looks fantastic." It's not difficult—only four words. She needs you to tell her that it looks great. Don't forget that your regular affirmation about her appearance means the world to her. It is the difference between her feeling beautiful . . . and the alternative.

But then there's the husband who doesn't notice. His wife asks, "So, what do you think?"

There's something you need to understand about this question. It isn't a question. Your wife isn't looking for your evaluative comeback. She's not looking for commentary on the merits (and demerits) of her latest hairstyle.

She wants you to say you think it's amazing and you love it.

Be generous with your compliments toward the efforts your wife makes to accentuate her best features. It's what wise and loving husbands do. You are literally helping your wife feel beautiful, and that is a wonderful gift for a man to regularly give his wife.

I'm glad our kids
h a v e   s u c h   a n
excellent role model.

Any encouragement from you about your wife's parenting is a great comfort. She's on call 24/7—even if she has another job outside the home. Moms are so close to their work as a parent that they can sometimes only see their kids' need for improvement, their own inadequacies as a parent, and what isn't getting done.

This affirmation is important because it contains not only deep encouragement but also a reminder that what is really going on is discipleship, which is exactly what a role model is doing on a daily basis. Mom often feels as though she's just hanging on and doing the bare minimum. Just about everything regarding motherhood says "You're not doing enough" or "You're not measuring up." Except she is doing not only a great deal but also a great job, and she provides an excellent example for your children. How powerful it is to hear from you that you believe she is doing a great job with the little souls God has entrusted to you and to her.

You are going to be an *amazing* mother.

The idea of bringing children into the world is intimidating for every first-time mother (and dad!). If the two of you don't yet have children, your wife may wonder, *Will I do a good job? Will I be a good mom?* She needs to know you have a great deal of confidence in her and you believe she will be a fantastic mom. She needs to hear how excited you are for her to be a mom because you believe she will do a great job. Your spoken confidence in her will fill her heart with encouragement and hope for a bright future with the children you bring into this world.

You know you are my
best friend, don't you?

Maybe you both know it deep down . . . then again, maybe not. Either way, this is something your wife will never get tired of hearing from you. Your strong statement that she is your best friend is like pouring love into her soul. Your wife wants a close "insider" relationship with the man to whom she pledged her life. In too many marriages, the years add only distance instead of closeness to the relationship. And this is a prospect that sends a cold shiver down her spine—not that it would happen to the two of you . . . then again, what does the evidence all around you suggest? Speak the words of intimate friendship to her by telling her often that she is your best friend.

I'm proud of how you handle **TOUGH** situations.

Life isn't all rainbows and butterflies. Some situations are downright frustrating, and your wife doesn't get a pass. She has to deal with the tough stuff of life too. When challenges arise that she has to handle directly, be sure to let her know you are proud of her. It's times like these when loyalty within your marriage trumps everything else and she will need to hear the calming sound of your supportive voice.

I don't know
w h a t   I   w o u l d   d o
without you.

You need your wife. What *would* you do without her? Be lost for a good long while! She is vital to the person you've become. Your lives have become inseparably intertwined.

This is a simple way of conveying a deep recognition of how important she is to you. She needs to be needed and you do need her, desperately. Tell her . . . and a warm hug to follow wouldn't go amiss.

You make me a
happy man.

She may be subtle or she may be out-front with her efforts to know, to understand you, but make no mistake, your wife is *constantly* observing to see where your relationship with her is in the present moment. *What's he thinking? Is he at peace in his heart? Is he happy? What's he feeling?*

I can't tell you how often I catch Lisa looking at me, so I ask her about it.

> Me: "Hey, what are you looking at?"
> Her: "Just checking to see if you are happy."
> Me: "Of course I'm happy!"
> Her: "Well, I couldn't tell, but I'm glad you are!"

This reminds me I need to communicate regularly with Lisa that I am happy and she's a big part of my happiness. She really does make me a happy man. She loves it when I tell her! Your wife will too!

I'm *amazed* at the woman you've become.

At some point, there will be a time when your wife hits a milestone in life. Maybe she chairs a committee in the local civic assembly, maybe she teaches a class, perhaps she becomes the go-to woman for biblical wisdom in the local church, maybe she completes her degree, maybe she becomes an entrepreneur with a successful business or gets promoted to some high responsibility, maybe the kids go off to college. Whatever it is, take the time to communicate to her that you are proud of her and of what she has achieved.

You are
my friend.

When you think of your "friend circle," specific names come immediately to mind, don't they? Would you include your wife in that circle? She greatly desires to be there.

Marriage is a multifaceted relationship. Yes, she wants to be your wife. Yes, she wants to be your lover. Yes, she wants to be the mother of your children. But one of the biggest dreams most wives have is to be close to her husband and to be his trusted friend.

Genuine, deep friendship can look very different from one marriage to another. You and your wife will forge a friendship unique to the two of you. On that journey, wherever it takes you, be sure to let your wife know you count her as your closest friend.

You are so
thoughtful.

Our wives have about a thousand things to think about every day—and they are often thinking about us! *What does he like? Where does he want to go? What would he like for his birthday? Would he...* She is a thoughtful lady. She considers and thinks about others. She thinks about you. Demonstrate that you see this wonderful quality in her by acknowledging to her that she is a beautifully considerate lady. Say to her, "I love how thoughtful you are."

Thank you for respecting me.

The man whose wife doesn't respect him is like a sailor without a ship. Respect—we need it from our wives like we need air. Your wife respects you in many ways, but it's something that is easy to miss. When you tell her you are grateful for the respect she shows, it signals to her that you are taking note, that you are feeling the respect she is giving. It's greatly encouraging to your wife to know you are aware of how she purposes to respect you. In so doing, you are validating not only what you see in her but also her obedience to God through the Word. Ephesians 5:33 says wives are to respect their husbands, and you've just acknowledged that she is walking according to the Word.

I'm *grateful* I can TRUST YOU with anything.

To be blessed to go through life with someone you can completely trust with absolutely anything is an awesome experience. Your wife wants you to know you can trust her and she wants you to put your trust in her. For many this is a very difficult hurdle to get over. Life teaches that to trust like this is to make oneself vulnerable and opens oneself up to getting burned. Both are true. But how does God describe His institution of marriage? He uses the language of total unity—the two shall become one. Live that oneness by telling your wife you trust her.

I have
t o t a l   c o n f i d e n c e
in you.

It made me sad recently as I heard a wife tell of the lack of confidence her husband had in her. She'd had a dream, but he had told her he didn't think she could do it, so she didn't . . . and seventeen years later, she still hasn't. Lisa and I both know she has everything it takes to do it. She could have "climbed that mountain."

A husband's words have great power. Sometimes that's the good news. Sometimes that's the bad news.

Does your wife know unequivocally that you totally believe in her ability to do "it"? Does she believe you have deep confidence in her capacity to achieve great things? God put the two of you together and told you, in effect, "Look after her. Nurture her. Cherish her." In great measure, your wife's confidence in herself will come from your confident belief in her. She needs to hear about the confidence you have in her, directly from you.

I'm
PROUD
to be your **husband.**

Do you see your marriage to your wife as a great privilege, given to you by God? We can have a lot of positive feelings and thoughts, but what good are they if they're only knocking around in our heads and hearts? Affirm your wife by telling her you are so proud to be her husband.

God knew what I needed. That's why He brought us together.

When a man acknowledges God and His sovereign place in his marriage, it's like he just wrapped his wife in a giant security blanket. Suddenly, that man is admitting that he is under authority, that he is accountable. He is not a law unto himself. He is also acknowledging that God is directly involved in his life through his wife in a positive way. And that is a blessing and great encouragement for your wife to hear.

I respect the *woman* you are.

In Christian circles, there is a lot of talk about how wives are to respect their husbands but far too little talk about how husbands are to respect their wives. Did you realize that a deep relationship is not possible without mutual respect? The man who doesn't respect his wife is in the process of destroying his marriage.

Yes, a man needs his woman to respect him, but she needs the *very same thing.* When you declare your respect directly to your wife, you are building her up in a way that, sadly, too few wives ever experience—and it's powerful! She has a deep need to be respected by the man to whom she has pledged her life. When a husband lives with a respected wife, he leads a blessed life. Don't miss out on this blessing—for you and especially for her.

My hat's
off to you!

Everyday life is filled with many moments when your
wife does something good. We're not talking here about
the "great" moments; we're talking about just the normal
good choices, good deeds, encouraging words offered to
a friend—the everyday good things your wife does. Perhaps she started a club or group of some sort, maybe she
decided to take up a sport, maybe she is the constant
source of support and wisdom for her peer friendships,
maybe she agreed to help on some community project,
maybe she made dinner for the zillionth time . . . all with
a smile. Don't let those moments go by without acknowledging them. Let her know you see the many things she
does to improve her self, encourage others, and bless those
around her.

You've got *great* ideas.

Of course I think Lisa has great ideas and has a lot to offer in any discussion, but does she know this all the time? No! How do I know this? Every time I acknowledge a great contribution she makes, every time I tell her I really value her thinking and love how her mind works, it's as if the sun shines just a little brighter. I think it all the time, but I need to remember to *say* it more often.

When Lisa started www.Club31Women.com, she was hesitant and apprehensive. "But I'm not a writer," she would say to me. But I believed in her in a way she didn't believe in herself. I knew she would have as powerful an impact online as she'd had in the lives of the many women she'd mentored. But knowing wasn't enough. She needed, and still needs, me to say it. To affirm her and encourage her by telling her I love her ideas.

Your wife will never tire of hearing how you appreciate her thoughts, ideas, and contributions. Be sure to tell her you value her intelligence.

You are such a *good woman.*

This comment applies to many different moments in marriage. When you're walking together through life, you can't help but see the many times your wife will make a selfless decision or a thoughtful choice for others, or do something kind for a total stranger. Don't let those moments pass without acknowledging that you see just how good a woman she is. After God's, there's only one voice of approval that's more important to her than anyone else's—yours. Don't miss an opportunity to tell her you see her goodness on display.

I rely on your
INTUITION.

Husbands could save themselves a lot of trouble in life if they would only stop being so cocksure about their own way of thinking and *listen* when their wives indicate a concern, a reservation, or distrust about a person, a great "deal," an idea or plan someone is trying to get you involved in, a business partnership, etc.

A woman's (your wife's!) intuition is often one of the most valuable, undervalued aspects of God's amazing gift to you. Now, for a guy, I'm very intuitive. But looking back on my life, I can clearly see when I should have trusted Lisa's intuition.

Like the time I bought four hundred beehives (when I had experience with only eight).

Like the time I trusted someone to help us and Lisa said she didn't trust that person.

Like the time . . . trust me, I could go on.

I can be slow on the uptake, but I'm not stupid! I've

finally learned to trust and rely on Lisa's intuition, and it has kept me from making many bad decisions.

Save yourself the trouble. Listen to your wife's intuitive observations—and tell her you rely on her unique perspective.

You're the *finest* woman on the planet!

Look for a moment today to come up beside her and whisper in her ear that you think she's the finest woman there is. It's a simple statement that, once again, lets her know you are single-minded and faithful in your heart. There's just nowhere else to look. Every wife loves to hear her husband's repeated statements of loyalty, commitment, and blind love.

I can
face anything
with you by my side.

You might have conquered mountains in the past or you might be doing it today or tomorrow. Whatever triumphs you have, whatever accolades you receive, whatever accomplishments you achieve, whatever challenges you face, one thing is certain: you didn't do it alone. Your wife was there with you every step of the way—fiercely loyal, always supporting, always encouraging, always sacrificing. What you did and what you face triumphantly was/is/will be because of the woman by your side.

It's often said that behind every successful man, behind every great man, is a good woman. You are who you are, in large measure, because she was there every step of the way. Tell her the powerful role she plays in the strength of your spirit to face life's relentless challenges.

Our kids love
(a r e g o i n g t o l o v e)
you so much.

Motherhood is looked at by the business culture, the feminist culture, and a broad cross section of the millennial generation as an impediment to achievement and a meaningful life. It's a degrading message to current moms and a discouraging shadow to future moms.

Motherhood is the "great giving" and often feels like a completely thankless job. Encourage your wife regularly in her role as a mother (or future mother) by speaking truth against the destructive, debilitating voices she hears on a regular basis. Remind her often of the love her kids have for her.

I don't deserve you . . .
but I'm glad
you're mine!

Seriously, do you deserve the woman God entrusted to you? Think about that. God says, "He who finds a wife finds a good thing" (Prov. 18:22 NKJV). So, congratulations, you are married! But did you truly deserve your wife or did God, in His great goodness and mercy, favor you with an amazing gift? When you tell your wife you don't deserve her, what you're really saying is that you think of her as someone of immense value. It's a message your wife will never tire of hearing.

I want to grow old with you.

With this one little statement, you are declaring your faith-fulness through the years. Ups and downs in marriage—they're guaranteed. But when you talk often with your wife about your desire to grow old together, you're giving her added assurance—a welcome reminder—of your commit-ment to go through whatever life throws at you together and to still be there, right by her side, as the years roll past. You're telling her that you're a faithful man—something the world is in short supply of these days but she will never have to worry about. Such verbalized commitment speaks warmth and security to the secret places of your wife's heart.

Thank you for being so good to me.

She is good to you—day in and day out, year after year.
When you take the time to count your blessings—given
to you by God through your wife—you begin to realize
just how good she has been to you. But realizing it is not
enough. You need to say it. You need to tell her how much
you appreciate the wife she has been to you. And here's the
awesome truth about speaking this way (with genuine sincerity) to your wife—it will increase her desire to continue
to bring that goodness to your life. In blessing her with
these words, you are blessing yourself. Smart man!

You're an *awesome* lover. I really enjoyed being with you last night.

Sex—it's God's idea (read the Song of Solomon). It's central to creation, and it's a big part of most of the years of a healthy marriage. And there's a lot for both you and your wife to learn about each other along the way. Truth is, there can be a lot of insecurity on both sides of the process. Your wife wants to please you. She wants to know she is meeting your needs. You want her to enjoy your advances and to desire you. Perhaps there's something you need to discuss with her, but don't forget that she may well have something she'd like to discuss with you. Her needs and desires may be different from yours, but they're just as strong in her as yours are in you, and they're just as important to her as yours are to you. Lead gently in that discussion. In the meantime, encourage her by taking the time to tell her you appreciate and enjoy her in bed.

I don't need
anything else —
just you.

The world is going to offer your flesh more ways to be unfaithful to your wife than there are grains of sand on the Oregon coast. Your wife needs to hear something—and she needs to hear it again and again, because she forgets. She needs to hear you say that she meets all your needs. When you tell her you don't need anything else but her, you're telling her you will look only to her to fulfill your needs and she can be confident in your faithfulness. And *that* is a very sexy message for any wife to hear on a regular basis!

I only have eyes for **YOU**.

You may not even realize it, but your wife can see—and feel—where your eyes are looking. Many men believe they are subtle, but it doesn't matter. She knows—a woman always knows if her husband is faithful or unfaithful with his eyes. And, of course, God doesn't miss much either!

Many have told themselves, "Yes, I love my wife, but I just can't help it. There are so many temptations." Those who believe that believe a lie—and that lie will destroy the security of every wife's heart it touches because it's nothing more than an excuse to keep on sinning and being unfaithful.

Strengthen your wife's dignity and security by telling her often that your eyes are reserved exclusively for her.

I'll always be *faithful* to you.

Faithfulness can be one of those subjects that never comes up in conversation because, after all, who plans on being unfaithful? At least at the beginning of the marriage? Yet unfaithfulness is about as common as BO on a New York subway in August—but not for you! Of course you are going to be faithful. You know it. She knows it. But it's still like beautiful music in her heart for your wife to hear you say it.

Embrace her, then look into her eyes and tell her, "I will always be faithful to you."

You never have to wonder where I am.

It's another way to remind her (she needs reminding because of the voices of self-doubt and because she forgets) that no matter who you meet or where you are—on a weekend away with the guys, on a business trip, at the gym working out, in the convenience store, wherever—she never has to worry about what you are doing because you love her and you are a faithful man.

Thank you for standing by me.

The fact is, at some point in your marriage, you will give your wife a reason to *not* stand beside you. It's easy to stand beside the husband who does everything right all the time—but that guy doesn't really exist, does he? Certainly not over the course of a few decades of marriage. For those who've been married for a while . . . remember those early years?

Sometimes the reason not to stand beside you will be something small and of little consequence. But, God forbid, there may be times when it's a big deal—a huge problem— that you created by a bad choice. Maybe you compromised your family's financial standing by a business deal gone wrong—or a thousand other things.

And there she was (and is, right now) . . . your wife . . . who took her wedding vows seriously—*in sickness and in health, for richer or for poorer*. She continues to stand by you because she's with you, all the way.

You are a blessed man. Tell your wife how much you appreciate her standing by you in the hard times.

You make me
feel like *a king*.

Every wife is a king-maker. She has the power to tear her husband down or build him up.

During those moments when your wife acts in a certain way or does something that makes you feel like a king, let her know. By doing so, you're also saying she is your queen.

You are a *great* cook/chef.

I cook a ton, especially since I got my Treager grill. There's nothing like taking a perfect rib eye roast off the grill after about six hours or a brisket or baby back ribs or a tri-tip or a New York strip or a pork shoulder. Oh, and then there's bacon. Have you ever had genuine smoked bacon? ☺

But wait, this is about Lisa cooking! And she is a *fantastic* cook. She didn't start out that way though. How did she go from zero to sixty in our first year of marriage? I didn't do everything right in that first year (can you believe it?), but I did this part right and so can—should—you, no matter how long you've been married.

But first, here's a story I heard recently that's way too common:

> When we first married, I was excited to cook dinner but wasn't that great. A mistake here, a complete disaster there, ten total triumphs in a row . . . it didn't matter. My husband always found something that needed improving. He wasn't

outright mean about it, but the constant message that I never got it right eventually took away my confidence in the kitchen. I didn't want to be a failure anymore and stopped cooking altogether. After the second year of marriage and to this day, he does 100 percent of the cooking.

This couple has been married for thirty-five years.

Now, if you like to cook (like I do) and want to do 100 percent of the cooking (like I don't) and your wife likes this arrangement, that's fine. But if you want to avoid the scenario of your wife dreading going into the kitchen and eventually not cooking at all, the power is in your hands— in your mouth and attitude, actually.

Even if she makes you a ham and cheese sandwich, tell her you appreciate it, it really hits the spot, it's so good— *say something positive*. Look for every opportunity to praise her and express gratefulness for her efforts.

So many men are far more critical and, consequently, far more destructive than they realize. Never criticize your wife's cooking—never!—and that includes all that "constructive" criticism (destructive criticism) you offer because you think you are helping. Trust me, you aren't.

Build her confidence by expressing your appreciation. Look for those opportunities and you'll find she will give Julia Child a run for her money in a few years.

And absolutely keep smoking/grilling your favorite cut of meat!

You're so *creative.*

Not everyone is married to a creative woman, but many are. For you, a simple recognition of your wife's talent in this area is a great encouragement to her. The truth is, her creativity is part of her person—part of her inner being. Indicating that you see her creative side and appreciate this part of her is another way of saying you value her. And what wife doesn't want to know her husband values her, not for what he can get from her but for who she is as a person?

69

I know you strive to please me . . . and believe me, *you're successful!*

Most husbands are oblivious to the fact that their wives actually spend time thinking of ways to please them. Unless you've been completely selfish and your wife's heart is closed to you, it's safe to say that every husband reading this book has a wife who spends some part of her day thinking about what will please you. So, first, recognize this fact about your wife. Second, tell her about it.

Don't know what to say?

If it's about physical affection, tell her, "You *really* satisfy me!"

If it's about managing the home (no assumptions here, just how most homes are run), tell her, "I just want you to know I am really satisfied with how you manage things in our home."

It could be about anything. The important thing is to tell her you are satisfied with her efforts to please you.

I *love* what you make.

A batch of cookies, a loaf of banana bread, lemonade on a hot summer day, dinner—or maybe she's an artist or a gardener or any number of things. A positive, encouraging word is so easy to give and so powerful to receive, and sadly, an opportunity so easily overlooked in the simple days that make up married life. Look for those simple, everyday things that your wife makes and use them as an opportunity to tell her again what you love about her.

You are one *talented* woman!

Without exception, every person is good at something. Everyone has a talent, a gift, for something. Your wife is no exception. Focus on that and tell her how talented she is. When was the last time you stopped to specifically focus on your wife's talents and to tell her how impressed you are? Praise from you is music to her heart.

You *never* stop
GIVING.

It's a cliché, but every woman knows it's true: a woman's work is never done. And a lot of that work is giving out and giving of herself to you. And that won't change until you are called home to eternity. That's why we shouldn't be like the guy driving his truck with his unhappy wife, her arms folded in frustration, staring out the window. "Do you even love me?" she asks. "I told you I loved you when I married you twenty years ago. If I change my mind, I'll let you know," he says.

Your wife never stops needing to hear that you see her and what she is doing and what she is giving. It warms her heart to know she's married to a man who notices all she does.

You look *fabulous* in that outfit!

Noticing . . . it's a huge part of communicating to your wife that you are thinking about her, you are connected to her, and her looks please you. Yes, she wants to look good, but she wants to look good for *you*! And if you never or rarely notice when she makes an effort to dress up (or even buys a new shirt or sweater), it takes most of the fun out of it for her. She bought it because she likes it, but she especially wants to know that you like her in it.

You make me *look good*!

Let's face it, men, the phrase "my better half" is true, isn't it? First of all, it is half-and-half because the two of you are one in God's eyes. How many times over the years has your wife made you look good?

And this isn't just about looks. How many times has she praised you to someone else for what you said or did?

How many times has she defended you when someone made a supposedly comical remark that was really a leveling comment about you?

How many times did she cover for you when you needed a little cover?

And then you walk into the room with her, arm in arm.

She really does make you look good, in every way. Be sure to let her know!

When you
walked into the room,
you took my breath away.

Life is full of planes to catch, bills to pay, groceries to buy, dishes to clean, laundry to wash, yards to mow. And then there's that dinner out, that wedding to go to, Christmas party to attend, that event you have to dress up for, and on and on.

Have you been married for one, three, five, ten, twenty, or more than twenty-five years? It doesn't matter.

She worked hard to get her hair just right, put on that fancy dress, and do everything else required to make things "perfect." And then she enters the room just before you two have to leave in order to arrive on time to wherever.

This is a critical marriage moment—a critical love moment. How will you handle it?

There's only one right way. Stop whatever you are doing.

Look at her for a moment in silence and then tell her she takes your breath away.

Haven't done this sort of thing in a while? Out of practice saying such things? There's no time like the present to begin to train yourself to see your wife the only way she should be seen by you in moments like these.

You are an *excellent wife* and I'm a **blessed** man.

It's a big, general, overall statement—and it doesn't need any explanation. It doesn't need to be delineated, parsed, or fleshed out. Just let it stand right there where you introduced it as a statement of the way you see things. And the only thing it needs to go along with it is a long, tight hug!

I *love* the home you've created.

Some men live with their wives in a dump, but they never take the time to consider the dumpy state of their marriage and its impact on their home. More often than not, the two go together. For most wives (not all), the state of her home is an expression of the state of her heart. And then there's the issue of managing a home. Keeping the wheels on the wagon is a whole lot of work! So find something your wife has created and then make a *big deal* about it! We husbands sometimes need to learn the grace of being genuinely grateful for many of the things we so easily take for granted. And gratitude tends to build on itself. When your wife experiences your genuine pleasure at what she is doing, it fills her heart with a desire to do more of it. This is a life principle that will transform your home into an oasis.

You work hard to make things *wonderful.*

It's true most of the time. She does work hard. But then there are those special times when she goes over and above to make the moment or event wonderful—family vacations, your children's birthdays, holidays. A lot of work is easily overlooked in the preparation and execution of these plans. At times, after all that preparation, she'll feel like she's out of gas. Your recognition and appreciation of all her hard work to ensure a wonderful time for everyone is like refueling at the gas station. Help your wife know you clearly understand and value all the hard work she's put in to make things great for everyone else.

The *Song of Solomon* has nothing on you!

This is just another creative way to tell your wife you enjoy having sex with her. She needs to hear you say it, especially as the years roll on. There will be times when she will ask herself in some secret place in her heart, *Does he still desire me? Does he still find me attractive? Does he still want me? Do I still turn him on?* Based on how attentive you are regarding these things, your wife will feel her allure to you is either constant or diminishing. You're playing a powerful, critical role here. Wise husbands understand this and enjoy the "creative benefits" that result!

I'm a
BETTER MAN
because of you.

It can seem at times that your wife is holding you back, is critical, is too evaluative, isn't on board, challenges your thinking, or questions your plans—and that's all super positive, even if it doesn't feel like it in the moment. How many times has your wife filled you with the desire to rise to the occasion? Got you to redirect your thinking about an important issue? Prevented you from making a bad decision? Encouraged you to think through your approach to a relational problem? It's true that she does make you a better man. She will be deeply encouraged to hear you openly acknowledge that fact to her. It's just one more way of expressing how you value her, and this in turn will strengthen the bond between you.

You are a *unique* person.

No two women want to be seen wearing the same dress at the Christmas party. And your wife doesn't want to be "run-of-the-mill," just one more nondescript entity in an ocean of sameness, the same as everyone else. This is especially true when it comes to your perspective of her. She desires for you to think of her as set apart, a cut above, special. Easily done! Tell her she is a wonderful, unique person. She's likely to ask, "Why do you say that?" not because she is challenging your assertion but because she wants to hear more about why you said so. Be prepared with an aspect or two of her personality that makes her the inspiration for your comment.

I'm *so glad* I married you!

It's a simple, sweet thing to say to your loving wife. But she isn't sweet all the time, is she? (Oh, and neither are you!) That is why this statement is all the more important. No matter what ups and downs you've experienced in your marriage over time, offering this comment from the heart covers it all—you're glad you married your wife. Your woman will love hearing this.

You'll *always* have my *heart.*

Let's be real. This world makes constant offers to steal a man's heart away from his wife. You know it, I know it, and our wives know it.

Tell your wife that she will always have your heart. Period. She'll never have to second-guess where your heart is because you gave it to her and will never take it back.

Making this statement is a bold declaration she will cherish. It's also a reminder in the face of temptation that you've made a commitment and wouldn't ever want to hurt the woman you love.

Your secrets
are safe with me.

You want your wife to be open with you. You want her to trust you. You want her to feel completely secure and safe with you, right?

She needs to know that every secret of her heart is safe with you. She needs to know that she can trust you to maintain a high, impenetrable security fence around the two of you, especially around the sensitive information she finds the courage to share.

Proverbs 11:13 says, "A talebearer revealeth secrets: but he that is of a faithful spirit concealeth the matter."

Your wife must be able to trust you completely. Tell her you are a faithful man and her secrets are safe with you.

God knew
EXACTLY
what I needed in a
woman.

Your wife and you both have strengths and weaknesses. And God is so specific in His plans that the two of you (when you're walking together in unity) perfectly complement each other.

There is going to come a time when it becomes crystal clear to you that the woman God gave you is *exactly* what you needed. That's the moment to let your wife know you understand what God was up to in putting the two of you together. Tell her how she perfectly complements you and how you see God's favor in His giving her to you.

Every wife desires to feel needed by her husband. God knows what you need—and you *do* need her! So tell her that you see God's perfect plan in which the two of you were meant to be together.

God is using you to help me mature as a man.

When we live with our wives in an understanding, respectful manner, they are given the opportunity to speak into our lives. Foolish, insecure husbands resist the corrective/evaluative comments and opinions of their wives. Wise men invite them. Yes, God wants you to be wildly happy and fulfilled in your marriage, but that's not all He intended in your oneness. He also intended that you mature as a man. If you choose humility, you will be able to see clearly how God has used your wife to help you mature. And it takes a mature, secure man to speak this truth back to his wife. Doing so doesn't make you weak (as this might feel to some). It makes you strong, and it will cause your wife to respect you all the more.

Be bold to tell your wife of this amazing role He has given her on your path to becoming a mature, godly man.

I wouldn't want
a n y o t h e r l i f e
than the one I am living *with you*.

Simple, settled, straightforward, and oh so comforting to your wife. Just to hear you speak of your contentment with her will make her heart smile. When your heart isn't roving, unsettled, discontent, and searching for other things, your wife enjoys the amazing freedom such security gives.

You are my
dream girl.

She knew she was your dream girl when you were dating.
You might have even used those exact words back then.
Does she still know it today? Have you stopped saying it?

Lisa and I have been married over twenty-five years.
I still love telling her she's my dream girl. It never gets
old, even though we are getting older. I plan on dating
my dream girl for the rest of my life. It's something every
couple can enjoy, but you, husband, must take the lead.

Of one thing you can be totally certain—she will *never*
get tired of being your dream girl. Tell her again what was
true in those early days of romance and you will soon find
that you are living them all over again.

You are a *beautiful* person, inside and out.

We don't (or we shouldn't) do things to get recognition or to make people conclude that we are a "good" person. Yet how powerful it is for a husband to tell his wife that she is a beautiful person, not just on the outside but on the inside as well.

In the course of her life, your wife will do many things that most others will never see or notice. But you are right there. It's important for the most important person in her life to speak words of affirmation, recognition, and approval into her heart—what an encouragement for your wife!

You are
so much fun.

It was our first year of marriage. Lisa was in the shower and there was a big pile of fresh, clean towels in our closet that needed to be folded and put away. I thought it would be hilarious if I buried myself in the towels, and when Lisa came in and reached down to get one after her shower, I'd grab her wrist.

Funny, right?

Wrong! Oh, so wrong! Boy did I get in trouble for that one!

So I've refined my approach and we've been laughing ever since.

In a great marriage, there are a lot of smiles and a lot of laughter. Don't let the work, the busyness, the stress, and the anxiety of your fast-paced life drown out and obscure the fun you have together.

Yes, life is serious. In the midst of it all, Lisa and I find the craziest things to laugh about.

Have you enjoyed a good laugh with your wife? Have you had good times together? There's plenty of time for the serious stuff in marriage. When you get the chance, tell your wife you think she's great fun.

You impress me, you *really* do!

If you and your wife have children, one of the best things you can do is send her on a holiday weekend for about three days and look after the children with no help (that's cheating!). Every husband who does this usually feels like he has been dragged through a knothole sideways and has an epiphany: *My wife is amazing!*

She also might be a great business woman. She might be an expert in any number of fields. Regardless of the accolades she gets from others, you matter to her more than anyone. And what you say matters more than what anyone else says.

Tell your wife she is one impressive lady.

You are one *sexy* lady.

Marriage isn't all about sex (despite what single young men think prior to getting married). In fact, it isn't all about any one thing. But sex is important for most of your married life, and your wife wants to know that you find her sexually appealing. She wants to know that you are still attracted to her. In today's language—that you think she's "hot."

Don't wait until you're undressed in bed with the lights out to express your sexual interest in your wife. Speak to her about her appeal during the day.

Now if you think God isn't into "hot," "sexy," and "steamy," you might want to check out what God has said about the subject in the Bible. Take away the euphemistic references to fruit in the Song of Solomon and you've got a solid R rating: case closed. God is into hot. It's not up for debate.

Though the years will continue to pass, one thing your wife hopes will not fade from your relationship is her sexual appeal to you. So speak to her about it in the everyday moments of your married life.

I *admire* you
SO MUCH.

Every wife has a deep desire to be honored and admired by her husband. They are simple words but pack real power in blessing your wife.

You're no *pushover*.
I love your spine of steel.

I'll let you all in on a little secret: I'm married to one strong lady. This is very important because of another little secret: I'm a little bit strong-willed myself (I know, it's a shock).

And I can tell you honestly that there have been times when I have been really frustrated with how strong she is. But the older I get and the more we are blessed to enjoy the years together, it has become very clear exactly why God put me with this strong woman. I needed her spine of steel alongside me in this ministry journey we've had these last twenty years. If she had the spine of a wet noodle, my personality would have run over the top of her.

A woman's strength is a man's great blessing.

Are you married to a strong lady? Recognize early the great gift her strength is. Recognize how necessary it is in your own maturity and development. And be sure to tell her how much you appreciate that aspect of her character (most of the time!).

You are a
considerate person—
of me and of
everyone else.

Being considerate of others is such a beautiful gift. Having a wife who is considerate of her husband is a God-given blessing.

Perhaps you are married to a particularly considerate wife. If so, don't miss the many opportunities to tell her you see how considerate she is and how much you love that about her.

Perhaps you are married to someone you wish was more considerate. First of all, make sure you are finding every opportunity to be considerate; and second, be sure to praise her every time (however rare) she demonstrates consideration. In so doing you will sow the seeds of encouragement that will, in time, lead to increased consideration on her part. That's how affirmation works—it brings out the best in all of us.

You're one in a million
...and *you're mine*!

True story of a first date:

> He looked into her eyes and asked, "Would you like to go
> out Saturday night?"
> "Sure," she said.
> As he stared across the table, he said with a serious, sincere tone, "You are one in four hundred."

End of evening. End of story.

The woman burst out laughing as she told me about this. "Really?" she said, laughing. "I was hoping for one in a million, but I didn't even make it to five hundred!"

No, your wife is one in a million, isn't she? This common phrase is another way to tell your wife she is unique, special, precious—like no one else—and remind her you are stoked that she is yours.

I'm a *rich man* because you are my wife.

The wise husband recognizes his wife's real value. He knows his life is rich and blessed beyond belief because of her.

Your wife desires to bring good things to you. She desires to do good for you. She hopes to be good to you. She wants to bring depth and richness to your life.

In the end, lots of money just doesn't matter. How do we know this? Because the richest people in the world are typically the most dissatisfied, unfulfilled, miserable people in the world.

What matters are the relationships we have. What matters most is the most important relationship we have, and for the husband, that's his wife.

True value and riches in this life are always found in relationships. When you tell your wife you are a rich man because of her, you're not only stating truth, you're communicating to her that you believe and understand her irreplaceable value. And that will draw her heart even closer to you.

I'd be *happy* with you
ANYWHERE!

This statement might not be technically true—what man, for instance, would be happy living in the middle of the Sahara desert with his wife? It's true, we all have our preferences. But this comment also contains a life-giving truth. The man who can say this to his wife understands she needs to know she is more important to him than anything this life has to offer. He's happy, just as long as they are together. Does your wife know this? Is she confident that you would be happy anywhere life took the two of you?

You make it all
w o r t h w h i l e .
I wouldn't want it any other way.

To know that she is enough, that you aren't wishing your marriage were different or pining away for something or someone else, is a great comfort to your wife.

There's a strong message of security in telling your wife you don't want a different life than the one you have together. It's a message she loves receiving from time to time because it brings peace to her heart.

I'll *love you* forever.

I tell this to Lisa all the time because it's true and I want her to think about my commitment. I want it to be in the forefront of her thinking.

It doesn't matter what life brings. It doesn't matter where the road of the future twists and turns. It doesn't matter what the world, the flesh, or the enemy flaunts in my face. It was true the day we married. It's true today. It will be true to the day I die.

Lisa, my Love, I will love you forever.

Matt Jacobson is the founder of FaithfulMan.com, an online ministry encouraging readers to love God and walk faithfully according to the Word. Matt is a biblical marriage coach and mentor and is co-host (with his wife, Lisa) of *FAITHFUL LIFE*, a weekly podcast focusing on what it means to be a biblical Christian in marriage, parenting, the local church, and culture.

Matt attended Multnomah University in Oregon and studied philosophy at Trinity Western University in British Columbia. For twenty-five years, Matt has been an executive in the publishing industry. For the past sixteen years, he has been pastor and elder of Tumalo Bible Fellowship, a thriving community of Christians with a purposeful discipleship focus on biblical marriage, family, and church leadership development. He is a marriage coach and the author of the bestselling book *100 Ways to Love Your Wife*. For more information, visit FaithfulMan.com/coach.

Connect with
Lisa and Club31Women!

Club31Women.com

Connect with
MATT and **FAITHFUL MAN!**

FaithfulMan.com

Hands-on advice
to *LOVE* one another better.

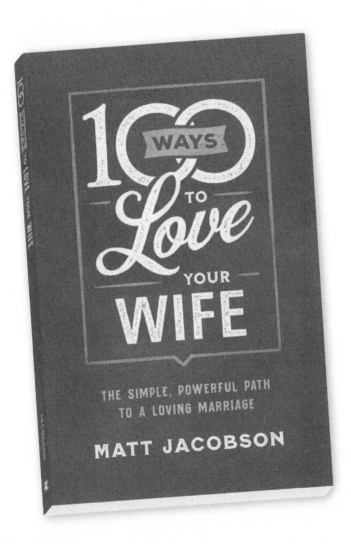

Hands-on advice
to *LOVE* one another better.

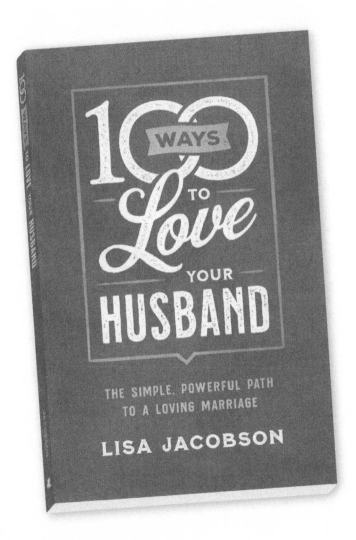

Encouragement to tell your husband *TODAY*.

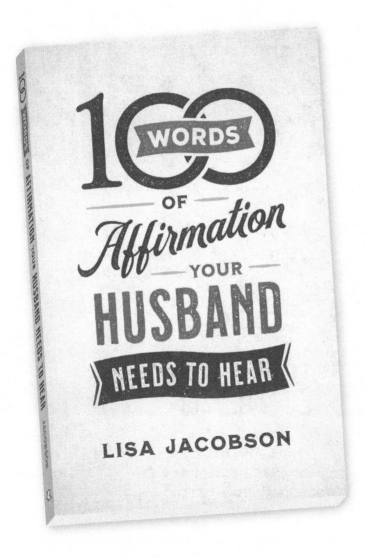

FAITHFUL LIFE

MATT & LISA JACOBSON

Welcome to *FAITHFUL LIFE,* a podcast where we pursue biblical Christianity on the topics of **marriage**, **parenting**, **church**, and **culture**. Biblical teaching, practical real-life instruction, and *lots of encouragement!*

Made in the USA
Coppell, TX
17 January 2022

71781405R10080